Fearless Follow-Up

Fearless Follow-Up

How to turn conversations into clients

SOMA DATTA

Wise Ink Creative Publishing
Minneapolis

ISBN 13: 978-1-63489-015-1

eISBN: 978-1-63489-016-8

To order, visit www.igsmgmt.com. Reseller discounts and bulk orders available.

Contents

Introduction

Since I started my own business in April of 2015 I've presented, coached, and trained people to network better. The more clients I worked with, the more they asked me, "How do I improve my follow-up?" I started to do more research, and I was shocked. I couldn't find a single resource to send my contacts that showed them **how** to improve their follow-up. Every article or book I read suggested to be effective in following up after networking a follow-up plan is necessary.

Ding ding! My brain lit up. I can write a book to show people how to improve their follow-up. Then I realized, I haven't always been good at following up myself. Before I started my business, I was an educational leader for the School of Business at the college level. At one of my performance reviews, my boss made it very clear. If I didn't follow up, and consistently, after my campus visits, I would derail my career. Ouch. My stomach clenched with fear then. In the first chapter of this book, I'll share with you how I overcame that fear.

Even now, I follow up well most of the time, but not all of the time. What is the difference? You should know that I love mysteries. Crime dramas on T.V. are my favorite because I love to watch the actors for clues and patterns to figure out who the killer is before anyone watching with me. In similar fashion, I set about looking for patterns in my follow-up. When was I successful and when did I…well…fail. I discovered I was most successful when I planned my follow-up before I even attended the event.

As a strategist, this realization should not surprise me, but it did. When I approached a networking event intentionally, with a plan, I followed up successfully and turned my conversations into clients. I composed the plan in my head, however. I needed the tools to plan quickly and completely on paper so I could follow-up well—consistently. It's these tools that I'm excited to share with you in this workbook.

It's no secret that writing down your goals into a plan increases your chances of success. Research continues to document the correlation between developing plans and business outcomes. A 2010 study published on smallbiztrends.com[1] reinforced the correlation showing businesses with a written plan were twice as likely to grow their businesses successfully as those who had no written plan.

Using the follow-up planning tools throughout this workbook you will create a plan to improve your follow-up exponentially.

Using the tools in this workbook you will:

- Define and envision the types of people you'll meet and what you'd like to learn from them.

- Establish a plan for giving and receiving value in your conversations.

- Collect cards intentionally to match your goals

- Segment your leads in a way that benefits you personally and professionally.

- Develop a record of the events that are meeting your goals and those that are not – saving you time and money

- Reflect on your networking efforts, track your follow-up, and grow your business.

I didn't want to write this book for us. I HAD to write this book for us.

1

1. http://smallbiztrends.com/2010/06/business-plan-success-twice-as-likely.html

1

Dream Forward for Successful Follow-Up

Whether you believe you can do a thing or not, you are right.
— Henry Ford

Beat the Fear with Vision

I'm not sure why I was surprised to discover I was most successful in my follow-up when I had a plan before the event. In my journey as an entrepreneur, I work with clients to clarify their vision of success before creating content or teaching tools. I talk to them about their team development goals before providing training. In each case, the end results meet and exceed my clients expectations. Why would successful follow-up be different? In this chapter, I'll start from the end by sharing what I learned, and then I'll show you how I came to my bit of wisdom, and finally share my vision for you and your success.

Vision + Proactive Planning = Consistent Follow-Up

This workbook is based on the formula above. To improve your follow-up, you need a plan that has a vision and is proactive. You will find activities, worksheets, examples, and trackers in this workbook, but no checklists. Together we'll create a **Follow-Up Plan** that will serve your needs over multiple events and years.

Business owners naturally understand the importance of effective follow-up to their success, and their bottom-lines. However, any individual at any point in their career will benefit from the tools in this book. I first learned to improve my follow-up as a State Program Chair for the School of Business at the college level. I didn't have sales goals as an educational leader, but my career did suffer because I failed at follow-up.

I struggled with following up after the campuses that I visited in my territory and my boss identified follow-up as a crucial need for my development. I knew I needed to do a better job following up after my campus visits, but I was overwhelmed by the prospect and afraid of what it would mean for my career growth if I didn't figure it out.

There were little to no resources to help me improve my follow up. I read, frequently, about how important it was, but could not find resources describing **how** to ensure that I did, indeed, close the loop. I went to my comfort zone – strategic thinking – and figured out plan.

First, I had to change my thinking. In my vision of successful follow-up, I wouldn't be "done" with my campus visit until I had sent a thank you email to the campus leadership that would include a summary of my visit, and action items from my meetings. To come to this mindset, I closed my eyes (yes, really) and dreamed about what successful follow-up would look like for me. I created a vision of my success and then planned backward to make it happen.

My job as a higher education leader required I visit ten campuses in Minnesota and North Dakota at least once every three months. At each campus, I met with at least three directors, admissions teams, student and career service advisors, faculty, and community members. That's a lot of notes and action items! With so much activity, I had to find a way to make the follow-up process easy for me to complete. It also had to be concise and relevant to my contacts. Finally, I had to create systems that were manageable, so I didn't overwhelm my schedule and could take action on what I'd promised.

How did I manage it? There are two main things that made a difference:

1. I changed my mindset. I decided I would consider following up as part of an event and not something that happened afterward.
2. To ensure I could follow through on my intentions, I created templates to help me plan, capture important notes and action items, and track what I completed and when.

My follow-up to campuses and the community improved instantly. If my travel took me to the Bismarck campus, and I knew I had a four-hour drive back to Fargo, I would plan a break about halfway through my drive at a location where there is wi-fi. A quick 20-minute break from driving allowed me to complete my notes and send a sincere email to the people I'd met during my visit. Done and done.

This *Dream Forward, Plan Back* process is the same one I use to help businesses grow today. It will also help you make the most of your networking events because when you plan for success you are more likely to achieve it. What's stopping you now is what stopped me – fear.

I didn't believe I could follow up quickly, concisely, and with a relevant message. When I returned from a visit, life and a landslide of emails would take over. I created this self-fulfilling prophecy ensuring ineffective follow-up. As an entrepreneur and trainer, I find my clients are experiencing the same self-fulfilling prophecy. Without a vision and plan for successful follow-up we feel:

- **Unfocused** – We wonder, with whom should I follow up and when? What should I do? How will I keep track?

- **Uncomfortable** – That unsettling feeling overcomes us. It's a combination of our minds telling us we should do something, but we're not sure what.

- **Overwhelmed** – The stacks of business cards from past events are still haunting us, and now we have more. Time away from the office means a flood of emails to respond to, and it's easy to overlook the follow-up we know we need to complete.

Your feelings of discomfort, lack of focus, and defeat – your fear – drives you to sweep follow-up efforts out of your mind. You may follow up haphazardly, or not at all, leaving potential clients to do business with competitors.

I want you to create a new prophecy, a new vision, for your success using this workbook. The changes you'll make are concrete, and the tools in this workbook will show you how. You can follow up with contacts from networking events quickly and easily, and **you've already developed the skills.** Now all you have to do is apply them to your events. You'll plan, prepare, and follow-through on your networking, turning conversations into clients.

How do I know the *Dream Forward, Plan Back* method will work for you? The framework I use in practice with businesses has roots in both communications and management theory. Let's look at what dreaming forward, or feed-forward means for successful follow-through.

Feed-forward in communication strategy

Think of feed-forward as the preview for a movie, the table of contents in a book, or the mood music and ambiance in a romantic restaurant. Feed-forward allows the communicator to prepare the audience for what's to come. Movie previews are carefully crafted and marketed to entice you to watch a movie, so ticket sales are successful. The table of contents of a book or magazine prepares you for the context and theme you will encounter. A romantic restaurant uses feed-forward to signal and reinforce the type of experience that diners want. In every case, feed-forward in communication sets the communicator up for success. At a networking event, you are the communicator.

Feed-forward controls in management practice

Feed-forward controls in management require forward thinking and solution orientation with the intent to anticipate problems and address them before they occur. Let me give you an example. In operations, a quality control manager might set a goal of one error for every 10,000 parts. In response, her team will set standards for equipment calibration and service. Each team member will receive the proper training. Her vision of success, one error out of 10,000 parts, resulted in a plan for people, equipment, and processes. She did not wait until there was a problem to fix. She used *Dream Forward, Plan Back*.

Because feed-forward control, and communication, is proactive and preventative, the management coaching industry has adopted it into practice as well. Feed-forward strategies work the opposite of feedback which can sound judgmental, "Did you do it right or wrong? Did you succeed or fail?" Instead, feedforward questions look like this, "How do you define success? How will you know if you're on track? What needs do you have? How will you meet them?"

What pure feed-forward practice is missing is the aspirational motivation that comes with **visualizing** the successful outcome you will attain. You will turn conversations from networking events into clients because you have a clear vision and a plan to make it happen.

I have a vision for you as you engage with this workbook. Imagine yourself spending time visualizing and preparing for your success. You'll focus on the people whom you can serve as you network and picture those contacts that can help you. Before you set foot in an event, you'll know your goals and objectives allowing you to approach the event with clarity, confidence, and excitement. As you make meaningful connections, you will choose the contacts with whom you will follow up. After the event, you will reflect on your experience, share your knowledge, add value to your leads, and develop a reputation for integrity through your follow-up plan. You will succeed.

Who Will You Meet?

Networking and follow-up are both about people. Planning for the types of contacts that build your knowledge and influence are an essential part of your plan. Customer, or client, personas are a critical tools for every business owner, sales professional, and networker to develop, track, and refine. Doing so will not only benefit you and your network, the customer intelligence you develop will help you add value to your relationships.

Relationships take priority as have conversations. You are not going to networking events to make sales. I'll repeat this because it's so important. You are not going to networking events to make sales. If this is your expectation, send me an email, and we'll have a little chat.

You are going to networking events to grow your influence. Yes, some of those relationships will turn into sales; in fact, effective follow-up is designed to facilitate bottom-line results – but not necessarily right away, and certainly not at the event itself.

Networking events are ripe with opportunities to learn about your contacts, your clients, and your competitors. To make the most of the conversations picture the people who would make great clients, valuable referral partners, and mentors.

If you are new to *customer personas,* you can learn more about them from a sales perspective in my blog post at http://igsmgmt.com/3-notes-to-scale-up-your-sales/ . I'd like to focus on how you would use personas to gather customer intelligence and focus your follow-up efforts to meet your networking goals.

At the end of this section, you'll find three worksheets to build baselines for your customer personas.

Customer personas – have them, track them, and refine them.

A customer persona, or profile, is a narrative description of your customer. Not everyone, as you know, is in need of your goods and services. Therefore, the purpose of the persona is to use words to illustrate a representative person who needs your goods and services to solve his/her problems. Using the worksheet for **Profile One**, describe your **ideal, or best fit client.**

Profile One: Define your best customer

Start with the person/client/customer who is most likely to buy from you. Take notes on the following:

- Where do they live and work?

- Is this person more likely to be a man or women?

- Into what general age range does he fall?

- Is she in the early, mid, or late career stage?

- What attitudes, beliefs, and values does he hold?

- Is she energized by networking? Does he avoid networking events?

- Why might she attend networking events?

- Who do you know that could help him be successful?

Once you've completed your notes, turn them into a story with your customer as the main character. Here's one of my personas focused on my teaching tools services.

Example:

"Terry has deep knowledge about his business and industry with a 20-year career behind him. Over the last several years, he's helped his organization grow, and in doing so, created many documents that help his partners, vendors, and customers. Currently, he has to be in front of his contacts to teach them to be a strategic partner, but he knows he could have a greater impact. Terry believes that his partners' success is tied closely to his success, but he's only able to influence those who live in the Twin Cities of Minneapolis and St. Paul. The organization's customers, vendors, and partners, however, are nation-wide. Terry enjoys the interaction that comes from networking events, but he feels spread thin. When he's talking to potential contacts, he's concerned about taking time away from his current network."

Please note that my clients are as likely to be men as women, but I used "he" to illustrate my persona. I could easily change all the pronouns to "she" and it would still help me target my message. Since gender doesn't matter, I used a unisex name. Try not to get too hung up on the gender specifics unless it's a significant differentiator of your service. If you're a midwife, you will primarily target women as clients. A barber might narrow his description with a masculine name.

Profile Two – Identify referral partners

A big part of serving your clients means adding value as a resource. **Profile Two** is reserved for your ideal **referral partner**. Keep in mind that you have the opportunity to meet a wide variety of people at networking events. Not all of them will be your client, but someone may have access to your clients in a way that you do not. Ask yourself the following questions to clarify this target:

- What kinds of people or businesses have complementary services to yours?

- To whom could you add value as a referral partner?

- What kind of people/businesses are in your network that would drive someone else's success? How?

- What kinds of goods and services would add value to your business as you serve your clients?

- What do your clients need that you don't provide? Who provides them?

- Who meets with people and businesses in your customer group on a regular basis? Why? What do they provide?

After you've taken the time to reflect on the questions above, develop a profile of one or two partners with whom you would collaborate.

Example:

"Anna's company sells promotional products. As part of her second customer profile, she discovered that making connections with event planners and speakers would add value to her networking efforts. The event planners are talking to businesses that could make use of her products (a referral for her) and event planners often need professional speakers (a referral she could provide.) By becoming a resource for speakers, Anna can add value to event planners she talks to, and together, they can both meet more people they need to be successful."

Profile Three – Learn and grow

The third profile worksheet is my favorite and is too often ignored while networking. With **Profile Three**, you will describe the person(s) who can **serve as a mentor or role model**. Think about the type of connections you'd like to make that will help you learn and grow, both professionally and personally with the following questions as a guide:

- What are three of my professional goals for the coming year?

- Which three personal goals will I prioritize in the coming year?

- What has peaked my interest? About what would I like to learn more?

- What are my top three strengths, personally and professionally?

- What is one area where I'd like to concentrate on improvement? (In addition to getting better at follow-up, of course!)

- What kind of time commitment am I willing to make toward my development?

- Are there particular channels of communication I'm comfortable using over others? (Consider in-person, email, Skype, telephone, instant messaging, etc.)

- What are some common qualities or characteristics of the people I most admire?

- How far am I willing to travel to meet with someone for professional development?

- In what ways could this contact be similar to me? Different from me?

The list of questions above is far from exhaustive, but it's a start. You might already have particular people in mind as you answer the questions. Regardless, I encourage you to create a more general profile. By writing down the type of person you'd like to help you learn and grow, you'll become more sensitive to the opportunities to meet new mentors or role-models you may never have considered.

You'll find the three customer profile worksheets at the end of this section. In section two, "Strategic Event Interactions" you'll revisit the profiles you created as you gather real-time customer intelligence at networking events. Taking time to reflect after events is a critical component of your follow-up plan. Don't forget to keep this workbook close at hand before, during, and after your events.

Have a Game Plan

When I was a kid, one of my favorite shows was *The A-Team*. I would repeat this catch phrase with the team leader, "I love it when a plan comes together!" He'd repeat this phrase after every successful mission. From the moment the A-Team met a client to their dramatic get-a-ways, they always had a plan. Now it's time to for you to put your **event-specific** game plan together.

I'm not a serious sports fan by any means, but I do understand the similarity in strategy between sports and business. Successful teams and organizations have both a broad, far-reaching mission and smaller goals and strategies to gain one win at a time. In my research, I found many articles and posts about a larger networking strategy. The component I found missing, and one that is critical for your Dream Forward Plan Back toolbox is an event-specific plan. It's not enough to know who you want to meet; you must be clear about what your intent is once you meet him or her. Whereas your overall networking strategy helps you choose the right events for your goals, a Networking Event Plan helps you focus your message to aid intentional follow-up.

If you have a vision of planning as a long and arduous process, don't fear. Once you've completed your personas, you can plan on the spot if needed. You may find an event opportunity presents itself unexpectedly. Take a few moments to jot down brief notes in your Networking Event Plan. It can make the difference between a successful event experience or a waste of your time and money.

Networking events that you've planned in advance, or take up considerable time or money, deserve a more thorough planning process. I've made it easy for you with the Networking Action Plan template. Once you use it and see the results in your success and follow-up, you'll never want to go without it again.

How to use the Networking Action Plan:

Event Name	Event Date/Time/Location	Cost
Fill in event name	*Record date, time, place*	*How much?*
Objectives	*Answer such questions as, "Why am I going to this event? What do I hope to get out of it? I'd call it a success if…"*	
Professional Goal	*What is one professional goal you'd like to accomplish?* *Example: Fine tune my ideal customer profile by better understanding business owners' strategic content needs. (Note: You may not have a professional goal for every event.)*	
Personal Goal	*What is one personal goal you'd like to accomplish?* *Example: Meet like-minded people who want to make a difference in my neighborhood. (Note: You may not have a personal goal for every event.)*	
Customer profile(s) in attendance	*Review your customer profiles. What types of people are attending? How do they align with your objectives/goals? With your profiles?*	
Must connect with/because…	*Investigate the people and businesses that will be at your event. What vendors must you visit? Why? Is there a potential partner, mentor, or competitor you'd like to talk to? What is your intention for these conversations? Who can introduce you to someone you'd like to meet? (Note: Keep your goals manageable. You don't have to meet everyone!)*	
I can be of service by:	*How can you be of service to the people you meet this day? How can you learn more about the needs of the people you meet? How can you help your contacts learn about your needs?* **Free resources that might help you can be found:** *People, articles, and other resources that might be of interest to attendees. Look outside your company and leave your sales pitch at the office.*	

If you're like me, there are events you attend year after year. Some networking events, like breakfasts or luncheons, are held monthly. Do you need to write your plan each time? Yes, yes you do. The reason a new plan is necessary is because many factors can change: your goals, the attendees, the stage in your business' growth, the topics, or the format.

Never take an event for granted or you might find yourself slipping into old habits that will sink your efforts at turning networking conversations into clients.

If you'd like to print out additional Networking Event Plan templates, visit www.igsmgmt.com/somas-books

Dream Forward Tools

Profile One: Define Your Best Customer

Use the following categories/questions to describe your ideal customer or client. You can read more about customer personas at http://igsmgmt.com/3-notes-to-scale-up-your-sales/.

Geographic Profile: Where do they live, work, and play. How about their customers?	
Demographic Profile: Consider the questions asked on the U.S. Census such as age, gender, income, education, household size, the age of kids in the household, life stage, etc.	
Psychographic Profile: What are your customer's beliefs, attitudes, hobbies, and personality?	
Pain points/solution: What problems are your customers trying to solve? How does your offering solve them? Focus more on need-based benefits than product/service features.	
Customer Persona or "Story"	

Profile Two: identify referral partners

Use the following categories/questions to describe possible referral partners.

Complimentary Services: What businesses offer complimentary goods or services to yours? What kinds of referrals do your clients ask from you?	
Access to Clients: What types of people or positions have regular access to your ideal client? Why?	
Add value: What contacts or resources would add value to your referral partner? What value would you like a potential partner to add to your clients?	
Describe the types of businesses would make a quality referral partner? (no more than two – you can add more in the future) What value would they add to your network? How would you support your partners' successes?	

Profile Three: learn and grow

Assemble your notes from the list of questions in the Profile Three explanation. Use the following categories/questions to describe possible mentors or role models.

Goals: What are your personal and professional goals for the year? In what one area would you like to concentrate your development?	
Exploration: What are your strengths? How can you continue to build on them? What would you like to learn more about this year?	
Motivation: What time commitment are you willing to make? How far would you travel to meet with a mentor? What channels of communication do you prefer?	
Find a Fit: What are the common qualities of people you admire? Which are similar and which are different from your characteristics?	
Describe the type of person from whom you'd like to learn. What would they do? Where would they work? What would you ask of them? What would you ask of yourself?	

To download additional profiles visit www.igsmgmt.com/somas-books

Networking Action Plan (Example)

Event Name	Event Date/Time/Location	Cost
Family Picnic (my favorite example)	*June 30, 2015, Soma's house, 12:00 p.m.*	*Potluck*
Objectives	*Spread the word to family and friends that I've started a new venture. Socialize and have fun. Eat my mom's barbecued chicken and fried rice.*	
Professional Goal	*Talk to my family about by new venture as an entrepreneur.*	
Personal Goal	*Graciously accept their congratulations and get comfortable with praise.*	
Customer profile(s) in attendance	*Potential clients – my cousin is a thought leader* *Referral partners – my uncle has written a family book* *Learn and Grow – my uncle*	
Must connect with/because...	*I must talk to my uncle because I'd like to understand his experience as he wrote, produced, and distributed a book about my Grandfather.*	
I can be of service by:	*Knowing how to talk about my business so they can understand what I do.* Free resources that might help you can be found: *N/A at this event, but who knows!*	

Networking Action Plan

Event Name	Event Date/Time/Location	Cost
Objectives		
Professional Goal		
Personal Goal		
Customer profile(s) in attendance		
Must connect with/because…		
I can be of service by:		

To download additional templates visit www.igsmgmt.com/somas-books

2

Work Your Plan

The essence of strategy is choosing to perform activities differently than rivals do. -Dr. Michael Porter

Staying Authentic with a Plan

I'm confident that you are thinking about networking follow-up differently than your rivals and peers do by now. It might seem odd to you to prepare so much before you've attended the networking event. It's okay to feel uncomfortable because you're developing a new mindset about how to follow up effectively. Although I'm suggesting you approach networking planning and follow-up differently, one important point about your networking should not change – be authentic with people.

This workbook is about follow-up and not the activities involved in networking itself since you can find hundreds of books on how to network like a pro. The best ones have in common two pieces of advice:

1. Be yourself.
2. Offer to be a resource.

How can you put the relationship first when you've filled out worksheets and templates before meeting anyone? Think of it this way; having a plan is not like having a script or a sales goal. Your plan is there as a gentle guide. You've anticipated questions, thought through your answers, and you have a vision for your success. I'll share three approaches my clients and I use to enhance the real-time networking experience and to support successful follow-up while having an explicit plan.

Gather and share information.
Leave the sales pitch for the sales meeting. Networking events offer an opportunity to learn more about the people in your community and industry. Ask questions and listen to the answers. When you feel a connection with someone at an event, share your needs with them as well. If they are networking to be a resource to you so sharing your needs is helping them, too!

Remind yourself of the value you offer.
Think back to the last entry in your plan. How did you want to be of service? What resources have

helped or inspired you lately? Offer to help the people you meet with an introduction or a bit of relevant information.

Practice positive self-talk.

When you change your language, you change your world. Positive self-talk is necessary when you're trying something different. Some changes in language can help you bridge your plan with your relationship building. Try these.

Before: I have to talk to one person from each of my personas.

After: I'd like to meet someone I can learn from today.

Before: If I don't (objective or goal from your plan) I've wasted my time.

After: My goals include (objective or goal from your plan) today. It doesn't look like I'll be able to accomplish that goal today, yet I can make connections and offer value to others during this event.

Having a plan before your event allows you to feel confident and prepared so you can relax and enjoy your conversations with people while you network.

It's a Conversation, Not a Survey

Imagine this; you approach someone that looks friendly at your networking event, and you introduce yourself. You shake hands, and then you begin firing questions at him or her. Yikes! Have you ever been at the receiving end of a scenario like this? Gathering customer intelligence and refining your personas can be part of a natural conversation. Instead of approaching intelligence as an interviewer, think of it as getting to know someone on a first date. You learn a little about him, and he learns a little about you. Keep it natural as you gather information.

My son Neil and I have the occasion to eat dinner alone once in awhile. He is 12 at the time I'm writing this book, so you can imagine I don't get too much one-on-one time to learn about his day and what he's thinking, learning, and feeling. Before our most recent meal together he says to me, "Are you going to interrogate me again?" What? Interrogate? I thought was being curious about his life and asking thoughtful questions. I told him so. Yes, he confirmed I asked "LOTS" of questions but I asked them one after another in rapid-fire succession. Due to the time pressure I felt I tried a little too hard. I'm learning to ease back on the speed and quantity of the questions.

Asking open-ended questions and listening carefully to the answers can help you gather information more naturally than I did in my dinners with Neil.

Questions you can ask:

- What brings you to the event today?
- What are you working on that's exciting?
- Is there a challenge you're facing in your job?
- How do you know the organizer?
- How can I help?

You might find the person you are talking to will turn your questions back to you; be prepared for a dialogue. Making connections takes time, and you won't meet everyone. In fact, some of my clients have the unreal expectation that meeting everyone is the way to make the most of a networking event.

Go back to your goals. Did you want to meet someone who could be a mentor or a referral partner? You could talk to five people and meet one who might be a good fit. That's success!

Reflect and Prepare to Follow Up

There is a sobering quote by Margaret Wheatly, an author and management consultant that reinforces the value of reflection to successful planning. She said, "Without reflection, we go blindly on our way, creating more unintended consequences, and failing to achieve anything useful." This quote describes how I felt about my follow-up skills before I worked on developing them. Reflection has become a core part of my plan. It's an important piece in my vision for your success as well.

The Event De-Brief worksheet included in this book has a spot at the top to write the date you intend to reflect on, and evaluate your networking event. If possible, try to take notes on the worksheet that same day as your event. If you don't have time, set your date for the next day and make it a priority. Consider scheduling it on your calendar.

What the Event De-Brief Does for You

1. Allows you to reflect on your objectives and goals, compare your expectations to results, and note any reasons for the difference.
2. Reinforces the value you offered to your connections during the event.
3. Prompts you to make notes about what you've learned about partners, clients, or competitors while it's still fresh in your mind. You'll appreciate your notes when it comes time to send a LinkedIn request, email, or handwritten thank you.
4. Provides a record of any surprises or challenges you faced while networking.
5. Helps you evaluate whether you would or would not attend the event in the future or whether you would recommend it someone else that would find it a better fit.

Debriefing after an event has many advantages. You can celebrate your effort, identify challenges, experience closure, and make better decisions.

Event Interaction Tools

Event De-Brief

Once you've completed your event de-brief, use your notes to refine your customer profiles or add to your customer relationship marketing (CRM) program of existing or potential leads.

Event Name, Date, Time, Location		De-Brief Scheduled	Cost
Objectives & Goals	Expected	Actual	Reason for difference
I added value to my connections by:			
What I learned about my customers.			
What my customers learned about me:			
Surprises and challenges included:			
I (would – would not) attend this event again because:			
I (would – would not) recommend this event because:			

Customer Intelligence notes

Summarize notes you've gathered that help you refine your customer intelligence. When time allows, add to or modify your profiles as needed.

Profile one: customer	New information: I met the following people, and I remember this:
Profile two: referral partner	New information: I met the following people, and I remember this:
Profile three: development	New information: I met the following people, and I remember this:

To download additional templates visit www.igsmgmt.com/somas-books

3

———

Beyond LinkedIn

*It's a dialogue, not a monologue, and some people don't understand that. Social media is more like a telephone than a television. –*Amy Jo Martin, Author of *Renegades Write the Rules: How the Digital Royalty Use Social Media to Innovate*

Many Faces of Follow-Up

It's time to make your vision of successful follow-up plan a reality. This chapter is designed to lay out your follow-up options, provide examples to inspire you, offers you tools to track your efforts, and helps you stay accountable to your vision.

The number of ways to connect and follow up with contacts after networking exploded with the proliferation of social media and it can be overwhelming. Do you still mail a physical thank-you note? What do I do after I send a LinkedIn invitation? Do people still get together in person? The answer to your questions is…YES! Below you'll find a summary of options you can use to follow-up after initiating a relationship, and some tips on when and how to use them.

LinkedIn

I know, the title of this section is "Beyond LinkedIn" but that doesn't mean you skip this step. The prevailing advice is to follow up with someone with an invitation to LinkedIn approximately 48 hours after meeting. Sometimes I make it, and sometimes it takes me longer. The trick is to do it.

Following up soon after you meet someone helps you to remember something personal to include in your custom invitation to connect. In the "Tools and Trackers for Follow-Up" portion of the workbook, you'll find examples to inspire you. Don't overlook your contacts' business pages, I'm sure they'd appreciate a new follower!

Thank-you notes

I do send handwritten thank-you notes from time to time. If there is a person with whom I've made a particularly strong connection, or if someone helped me fulfill a need immediately at the event, I send a handwritten note. There is something so intimate about your handwriting versus an email. It makes my day when I receive a note that is brief, heartfelt and recalls a shared detail.

Email

I use email to follow up on a specific action I promised while meeting someone; for example, if I mentioned an article or resource I thought he/she would appreciate, I'll send it via email. I could send it through LinkedIn mail. However, we may not have connected yet. By sending an email I convey the message that I'm not expecting anything in return, I'm simply fulfilling my promises.

Twitter, Google, Facebook

If you're still getting to know prospects or contacts and want to learn more about what drives and motivates them, follow them on Twitter, run a Google search, or Like their Facebook pages. Resist asking for a return Follow or Like. Once they get to know you, they may reciprocate, but that's not the point. Your goal is to get to know their attitudes, beliefs, personality, likes and dislikes. Social media has no shortage of this relevant information.

Let's talk

Following up by phone or requesting a personal meeting is always an option. Follow these pointers to respect your contacts' time, and maximize your own:

1. Be clear about why you want voice/face time. If you're hoping for a sale, but you've asked for a 15-minute phone call to "talk about ways you can work together" you've set yourself up to lose a potentially beneficial relationship.

2. Communicate your intention honestly with your contact. I called an event planner I met at a speaking engagement after she complimented me on my presentation. In my email, I asked for 15 minutes to gather feedback from her so I could continue to learn and improve as a speaker. Even after setting this expectation, she said with guilt during the call, "I don't have an event to hire you for right now." I had to assure her I was simply seeking feedback at this time. I didn't expect a job!

3. Be where you say you'll be when you said you'd be there. Doing what you say you'll do is the essence of integrity—the foundation of every meaningful relationship. If you said you'd call Wednesday at 10 a.m., make the call. If you asked for 30-minutes, don't go over time without asking for permission. Professional courtesy reigns.

It's a Marathon, Not a Sprint

When I gave myself permission to be focused in my networking and selective in the cards I collect, my follow-up improved tremendously. Now I view networking and follow-up as a continuous rhythm instead of a one-time act. You may have heard the phrase, "Life is not a sprint, it's a marathon." The same holds true for follow-up after networking.

How to make the marathon work for you:

Keep your follow-up manageable – I've mentioned this throughout the workbook, and it bears repeating. Trying to meet and follow up with everyone at a networking event is improbable. Even if you attend a small group workshop with four other people, you don't need to give each contact you've made the same kind of attention.

Segment your leads – You segmented your customers through profiles before the event, now it's time to segment your leads. In addition to the profile or persona in which your prospects belong, you'll also segment them based on what they need and want from you today. In the trackers I've provided in the "Tools and Trackers" section are filled with lines ready to capture your contacts. When I use the trackers, I might have one or two contacts in each category for a large event. The purpose of the tracker is to add to your lists and follow through as you attend multiple events throughout the year. The trackers represent your marathon. Sort your leads into three categories to keep the pace to success:

- *Engage with Resources* – You have the most to learn about the contacts on this list. However, during your conversations you've discovered you have valuable resources to share with them. As you share, take steps to learn more about their needs. Tip – Give selflessly

- *Learn, Grow, Refer* – You had a great conversation and made an authentic connection with someone from whom you can learn, or someone you're excited to refer to others. Keep track of who they are and learning or referral opportunities.

- *Opportunity is Imminent* – We all hope to fill this bucket. However, the leads in this category take time and effort to develop. If you've happened across someone who is ready to buy today or is open to a sales meeting, then he/she belongs in this tracker. More often, you'll see movement from the first two categories into this one. When a lead in the "Engage with Resources" tracker becomes a qualified contact, move it down to the appropriate category and use the tracker to keep on top of your activity.

Keep your favorite resources at your fingertips:

Imagine this scenario. You learn your contact has an interest in (enter topic here). You remembered seeing a post or article last week, but you can't recall from where. The next 30-minutes to an hour you search online and offline to find it and send it to your contact as a resource to engage with him/her. This scenario used to happen to me all the time; then I started using the Resources Tracker I've shared with you in the next section. All the tools in this workbook are designed to work together seamlessly and support your vision for successful networking.

Tools and Trackers for Follow-Up

Examples of written follow-up communication

Thank-you notes

Quality thank-you notes have four factors in common: the thank you, a desire to stay in contact, a concrete detail about the experience, and an authentic compliment. For a big impact, write your note by hand.

Example

Dear (Name),

I appreciate the time you spent with me today talking about a new business venture. It's exciting to see the product up close, and customizing the prototype colors to match my brand was a delightful touch I won't soon forget.

Thank you for taking the time to invite me to your business, so I can better refer your services to others. I look forward to taking the next steps in our partnership.

Sincerely,
(Your name)

Emailing a resource

Keep track of your favorite resources with the follow-up trackers in the next section. When it's time to send useful information to a contact, you'll be able to quickly find just the right article.

Example
Subject line: Great meeting you (the day), I thought you'd be interested in (name of article/resource)

Hi (name),

It was wonderful to meet you at the (name of event) on (date). I remember you talked about how you're facing the challenge of expressing the value of promotional items to potential clients.

I'm (attaching, linking to...) this resource on just that topic that I thought you'd find useful. I'd like your feedback on whether it would help you better explain your company's value.

Please let me know if there is anything else I can do for you.

(your name)

Customize your LinkedIn message

Too many people fall back on the ease of sending the pre-populated LinkedIn message for new connections. Customizing your message is worth the time, even after you've met many people at a conference. Keep it short and relevant.

Example

Subject line: Our conversation about (topic) stuck with me

Hi, (name).

I enjoyed our conversation about (topic) at the (name of event) on (date). When I returned, I saw this (resource, tip, news, idea) and thought of you.

I'd love to hear if you find it useful. Will you connect with me on LinkedIn so we can continue our discussion?

(your name)

Voicemail

Build your credibility in the 30-seconds after the beep. Articulate your name clearly, leave your phone number, keep it short, use their name, and use a conversational but professional tone. Prepare and practice, but resist reading from a script.

Example

Beeeep

Good morning, (contact's first name). This is (your first and last name) calling. I enjoyed talking to you about the new projects you have coming up at the (name of event) on (date). Since our responsibilities have so much in common, I'd love to talk more about how you're entering new markets. I'm available on Wednesday and Thursday morning for a phone call next week. Could you spare 30 minutes? My number is xxx-xxx-xxxx. I look forward to hearing from you.

Follow-Up Tracker

Event name, date, time, location:

Engage with resources						
Name	Company	Memory/Impression	Action(s) to take	LI	FB	Resources

Learn, Grow, Refer

Name	Company	Memory/Impression	Role	LI	FB	Refer to

Opportunity is Imminent

Name	Company	Memory/Impression	Pain/Benefit	LI	FB	Call? Meet? Send Info?

Resources Tracker

Use this tracker to record the resources and feedback on the topics of greatest interest to you and your contacts.

Topic one:

Go to resources:

Sent to:

Feedback:

Topic two:

Go to resources:

Sent to:

Feedback:

Topic three:

Go to resources:

Sent to:

Feedback:

Topic four:

Go to resources:

Sent to:

Feedback:

To download additional templates visit www.igsmgmt.com/somas-books

4

Vision Realized

As a conclusion to this workbook, I'd like to revisit our use of *Dream Forward, Plan Back* to take the fear out of follow-up and help you turn conversations into clients.

Dream Forward

Using this workbook will allow you to visualize your successful follow-up plan. You will know who to engage, how to provide value, and where you want to grow your influence. You will attend networking events with clarity and confidence allowing you to focus on the relationships you are building. You will build integrity with your contacts by following up personally and consistently in a way that adds value your relationship. You will succeed.

Plan Back

From the tools and resources in this workbook you are able to articulate the value of vision and planning in your networking success. You can identify and describe three segments of contacts that can help you and your business grow. You have the tools to plan your goals for specific events, reflect on your networking efforts, and implement and track your follow-up plan.

As I'm writing this conclusion, I'm smiling and glowing. "I love it when a plan comes together."

About the Author & About Intentional Growth Strategies

Soma's eight years teaching in and managing the School of Business Program for Rasmussen College in MN and ND ensures strong curriculum design, professional training, and focused strategy behind your company's growth plans. A passionate educator of adult students in undergraduate education, Soma, knows how to turn your ideas into tools that engage, inspire, and produce results.

Soma's degree in creative writing and MBA in Marketing provides you an unprecedented balance between personalization and profit. Our founder puts her 20 years experience in marketing and management for companies large (General Mills) and small (Minnesota Parent Magazine) together with expertise in professional communication and story-telling, so you make the most of every customer engagement.

About Intentional Growth Strategies

Mission

Intentional Growth Strategies brings to life the ideas of small business owners and industry experts, helping them sell more by turning their experience into business-generating content and teaching tools that benefit their customers. With the power of B-school expertise at work for our clients, we are insistent that the content creation and course design principles we propose rigorously follow industry and higher education standards.

Fearless Follow-Up Training

We offer a full suite of training to build your skills, or those of your team, to meet your company's mission. Contact Soma for keynote addresses or custom training designed to transfer learning into action. Our founder uses the tools she's gained through teaching and developing in-person and online classes, to engage all participants in active learning. We learn best when we have fun…so let's have fun.

Visit www.igsmgmt.com/services to learn more.